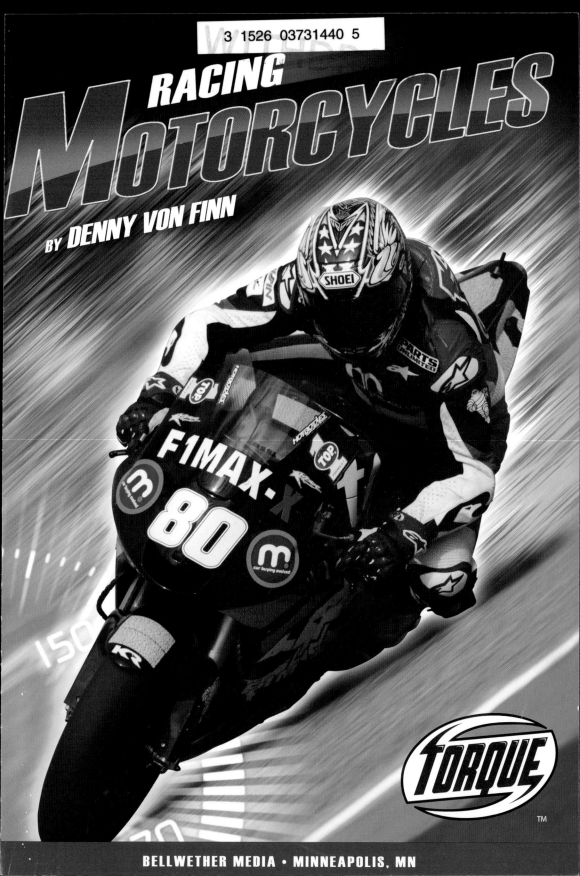

RACING
MOTORCYCLES

BY DENNY VON FINN

TORQUE

TM

BELLWETHER MEDIA • MINNEAPOLIS, MN

TM

Are you ready to take it to the extreme?
Torque books thrust you into the action-packed world
of sports, vehicles, and adventure. These books may
include dirt, smoke, fire, and dangerous stunts.
WARNING: read at your own risk.

This edition first published in 2010 by Bellwether Media, Inc.

No part of this publication may be reproduced in whole or in part without written permission of the publisher.
For information regarding permission, write to Bellwether Media, Inc., Attention: Permissions Department,
5357 Penn Avenue South, Minneapolis, MN, 55419.

Library of Congress Cataloging-in-Publication Data

Von Finn, Denny.
  Racing motorcycles / by Denny Von Finn.
    p. cm. – (Torque. The world's fastest)
  Includes bibliographical references and index.
  Summary: "Amazing photography accompanies engaging information about racing motorcycles.
The combination of high-interest subject matter and light text is intended for students in grades 3 through 7"
–Provided by publisher.
  ISBN 978-1-60014-291-8 (hardcover : alk. paper)
  1. Motorcycles, Racing--Juvenile literature. I. Title.

  TL442.V66 2010
  629.227'5--dc22

                              2009013762

CONTENTS

What Are Racing Motorcycles?

Racing motorcycles are two-wheeled vehicles with powerful engines. They are also lightweight. This gives them an excellent **power-to-weight ratio**.

Racing motorcycles are designed for specific types of performance. Some racing motorcycles are built to go fast in a straight line. Others can handle tight turns at incredible speeds.

Drag bikes race on **dragstrips**. Riders reach speeds of 200 miles (322 kilometers) per hour or more. The race is just 1,320 feet (402 meters), but riders need up to 1 mile (1,600 meters) to stop!

Land-speed motorcycles also race in a straight
line. Riders take turns on a 1-mile (1.6-kilometer)
course. Each hopes to record the fastest time.
The **Bonneville Salt Flats** is a famous spot for
land-speed races.

Some motorcycles are designed for road racing. These races are different than drag races and land-speed racing. Several riders race against one another on tracks with twisting corners. These bikes reach speeds over 200 (322 kilometers) miles per hour. In 2008, a road racer went over 215 miles (346 kilometers) per hour on a Ducati motorcycle.

9

Racing Motorcycle Technology

Racing motorcycles have special features to help them go fast. A drag bike is built on a **chassis** made of lightweight metal. A sleek body helps the bike cut through the wind. Large **V-twin** and **inline** engines power drag bikes. Some drag bike engines burn **nitromethane**. This creates even more power.

Fast Fact

Larry "Spiderman" McBride reached 248 miles (399 kilometers) per hour on his drag bike in 2006.

Fast Fact

Rocky Robinson's twin-engine motorcycle reached nearly 361 miles (581 kilometers) per hour at Bonneville in 2008.

Land-speed motorcycles come in many shapes and sizes. Engines range from 50 **cubic centimeters (cc)** to 3,000cc. Some motorcycles have more than one engine. Rocky Robinson's Top 1 Ack Attack has two engines. Some land-speed motorcycles look like missiles. A sleek body surrounds the bike and rider. It lets the bike move easily through the air.

Road-racing motorcycles look much like the **sport bikes** seen on public roads. These racing bikes have many types of engines. Engines with four **cylinders** are the most popular for road racing.

Road-racing bikes are built with lightweight materials such as **carbon fiber**. Electronics control how much fuel is sent to the engine cylinders. These motorcycles can accelerate from 0 to 100 miles (160 kilometers) per hour in around 3 seconds!

Road-racing motorcycles do more than thrill racing fans. Motorcycle companies use these motorcycles to test new features for their sport bikes. Some features enjoyed by racers are later used on the motorcycles sold to the public. These features may increase the performance and the safety of **streetbikes**.

The Future of Racing Motorcycles

Many people are worried about gasoline engines. Gasoline is expensive and it pollutes. Manufacturers are looking to **green technology** to power racing motorcycles. They are designing electric engines. These engines pollute much less than gasoline engines. The Mission One motorcycle is an electric racing bike. It can go 150 miles (252 kilometers) per hour!

Hydrogen power is another green technology. The ENV is a hydrogen-powered streetbike. It pollutes less than gasoline-powered motorcycles. However, its top speed is only 50 miles (80 kilometers) per hour.

Manufacturers hope to soon use hydrogen power in racing motorcycles. They want to create fast, low-pollution bikes to thrill racing fans!

GLOSSARY

Bonneville Salt Flats—a huge, flat area in Utah where racers gather for land-speed events

carbon fiber—a material made of strong fabric mixed with hardened plastic

chassis—a metal frame on which a motorcycle's engine, seat, and rear wheel are mounted

cubic centimeters (cc)—the most common measurement used to describe the size of motorcycle engines

cylinders—the hollow, can-shaped areas of an engine where fuel explodes to create power

dragstrips—the straight two-lane tracks where drag bikes compete against each other

green technology—technology that is environmentally friendly

hydrogen power—power taken from hydrogen gas

inline—an engine design with cylinders arranged in a row

nitromethane—an explosive liquid that helps power some drag bikes

power-to-weight ratio—an engine's power divided by the weight of the motorcycle

sport bikes—motorcycles designed for high speeds and excellent handling

streetbikes—motorcycles used on public streets and roads

V-twin—a motorcycle engine design with two cylinders arranged in the shape of the letter V

TO LEARN MORE

AT THE LIBRARY

David, Jack. *Sport Bikes*. Minneapolis, Minn.:
Bellwether Media, 2008.

Dubowski, Mark. *Superfast Motorcycles*. New York, N.Y.:
Bearport, 2005.

Hofer, Charles. *Motorcycles: The World's Fastest Machines*. New York, N.Y.: PowerKids Press, 2008.

ON THE WEB

Learning more about racing motorcycles
is as easy as 1, 2, 3.

1. Go to www.factsurfer.com.

2. Enter "racing motorcycles" into the search box.

3. Click the "Surf" button and you will
   see a list of related Web sites.

With factsurfer.com, finding more information is just a
click away.

INDEX

The images in this book are reproduced through the courtesy of: digitalsport-pho-toagency, front cover; afaizal, pp. 4-5; Rusty Jarrett / Stringer / Getty Images, p. 6; Frank Kletschkus / Alamy, pp. 7, 12-13; Lario Tus, pp. 8-9; Phillip W Hubbard, pp. 10-11; Tony Pleavin / Alamy, pp. 14-15; Yamaha Motor Corporation, pp. 16-17; Mission Motor Company, pp. 18-19; Justin Sullivan / Getty Images, pp. 20-21.